WORSHIP QUEST WORKBOOK

WORSHIP QUEST WORKBOOK

A Study Guide for the Book by Steven D. Brooks

CHRIS C. MONROE

FOREWORD BY
STEVEN D. BROOKS

WIPF & STOCK · Eugene, Oregon

WORSHIP QUEST WORKBOOK
A Study Guide for the Book by Steven D. Brooks

Wipf & Stock
An Imprint of Wipf and Stock Publishers
199 W. 8th Ave., Suite 3
Eugene, OR 97401

www.wipfandstock.com

PAPERBACK ISBN: 979-8-3852-2994-9
HARDCOVER ISBN: 979-8-3852-2995-6
EBOOK ISBN: 979-8-3852-2996-3

08/05/25

Be sure to check out Worship Quest Ministries

Encouraging worship renewal and spiritual formation for the global Christian church

worshipquest.net

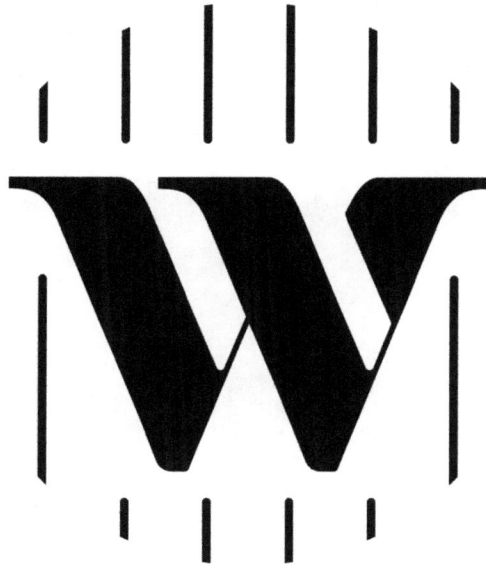

Contents

PART FOUR. ROLES OF WORSHIP LEADERSHIP

Foreword

I'M PLEASED TO INTRODUCE this Workbook as a companion to the 2ⁿᵈ Edition of my book, *Worship Quest: An Exploration of Worship Leadership*. From the very beginning, my desire in writing *Worship Quest* was to provide a resource that would help worship leaders, pastors, church musicians, creatives, and congregations engage in a deeper exploration of worship and its leadership within the life of the church.

Chris Monroe has taken this vision a step further by crafting this Workbook that invites readers into meaningful reflection, discussion, and practical application. His commitment to helping others think deeply about worship and his passion for equipping those who serve in worship leadership are evident throughout these pages. With thoughtful questions, insightful supplemental content, and space for reflection, this Workbook encourages both individuals and groups to journey through *Worship Quest* in a way that is engaging, transformational, and applicable to their unique contexts.

I am deeply grateful for Chris' work and his heart for strengthening the church's understanding and practice of worship. I appreciate how this resource serves as a tool for individuals seeking to grow in worship leadership, as well as for groups—such as worship teams or Bible study classes—interested in deepening their understanding of worship. If you are a worship leader or pastor engaging with these pages, I pray this Workbook will challenge, inspire, and equip you to lead worship with greater theological depth, pastoral sensitivity, and creative imagination. For those using this Workbook with a group or team to deepen your church's understanding of worship, may this study guide serve you well as you seek to glorify God and worship him in spirit and truth.

STEVEN D. BROOKS
Author, *Worship Quest*

How To Use This Workbook

THIS WORKBOOK IS DESIGNED to be a helpful tool for use alongside the 2nd Edition of *Worship Quest: An Exploration of Worship Leadership*, by Steven D. Brooks. It is not a replacement for and does not contain the text of the *Worship Quest* book. The Workbook is intended to be a supplemental resource, helping readers and students engage with the content and ideas addressed in *Worship Quest* in order to deepen one's understanding of the book and the material that Steven Brooks presents.

The Workbook begins with a series of questions you are encouraged to answer before reading each chapter in the *Worship Quest* book. These questions are intended to get you thinking about each topic before diving into a journey of discovery you'll encounter in each chapter that Brooks addresses.

The Workbook is organized chapter by chapter. After reading each chapter, the Workbook will guide you through a series of questions to help you deepen and benefit from the material in that chapter. I encourage you not to rush, but to take the time necessary to thoughtfully, honestly, and thoroughly answer each question. Although ample space is provided to write down your answers, you may want to have extra paper on hand for this purpose.

Written in connection to many of the questions, the Workbook contains summary observations meant to help you zero in on the topics Brooks presents. Each Workbook chapter also features additional content, included to further enrich your learning journey through the *Worship Quest* book. These features include a section entitled, *More To Think About*—which presents thought provoking ideas, consistent with each topic you'll encounter in *Worship Quest*, as well as *Wisdom From The Early Church*—inspiring quotes from a variety of early church writings. Each chapter in the Workbook also ends with a *Closing Prayer*, and the opportunity for you to prayerfully fill-out a personal *Action Plan Commitment*. I strongly urge you to fill out each of these commitments in order to take what you have learned from the *Worship Quest* book and Workbook, apply it to your own life and ministry, and then use them as a tool to hold yourself accountable.

It is an honor and a joy for me to help guide your journey through *Worship Quest: An Exploration of Worship Leadership*, by Steven D. Brooks. I trust that, together, his book and this Workbook will be a blessing to you and all who serve in the worship of our Triune God!

CHRIS C. MONROE, DWS

Questions to Answer Before Reading Each Chapter

BEFORE READING CHAPTER 1:

When you hear the word *worship*, what's the first thing that enters your mind?

_____

_____

_____

_____

_____

If someone asked you to define worship, what would you say?

_____

_____

_____

_____

_____

BEFORE READING CHAPTER 2:

What would you consider to be idolatry?

_____

_____

_____

_____

_____

Is belief in the Trinity important? Why or why not?

_____

_____

_____

_____

_____

BEFORE READING CHAPTER 3:

Are some places more appropriate for worshiping God than others? Why?

_____

_____

_____

_____

_____

BEFORE READING CHAPTER 4:

If someone asked you *why* we should worship God, what reason would you give them?

_____

_____

_____

_____

Is there a wrong reason for worshiping God, and if so, what might that be?

_____

_____

_____

_____

_____

BEFORE READING CHAPTER 5:

Is there anyone who might be disqualified from worshiping God? Explain.

_____

_____

_____

_____

_____

BEFORE READING CHAPTER 6:

Are there any correct ways to worship God, and if so, what are they?

_____

_____

_____

_____

_____

BEFORE READING CHAPTER 7:

Do you worship the Lord completely by yourself? If so, when, where, and how often?

_____

_____

_____

_____

_____

BEFORE READING CHAPTER 8:

Why is worshiping with other believers important?

_____

_____

_____

_____

_____

BEFORE READING CHAPTER 9:

How should Christian worship affect how we live our lives?

_____

_____

_____

_____

_____

BEFORE READING CHAPTER 10:

What should the private worship of God look like?

_____

_____

_____

_____

_____

BEFORE READING CHAPTER 11:

What might the benefits be of worshiping God with a small group of people?

_____

_____

_____

_____

_____

BEFORE READING CHAPTER 12:

What expectations should we have when an entire congregation worships together?

_____

_____

_____

_____

_____

BEFORE READING CHAPTER 13:

What might the benefit be of multiple congregations gathering to worship God together?

_____

_____

_____

_____

_____

BEFORE READING CHAPTER 14:

When someone says God "called" them into a ministry, what do they mean?

_____

_____

_____

_____

_____

BEFORE READING CHAPTER 15:

Who is the most effective Worship Leader you personally know, and what makes them so?

_____

_____

_____

_____

_____

BEFORE READING CHAPTER 16:

Since most people can at least sing, what enables someone to lead others in singing?

_____

_____

_____

_____

_____

BEFORE READING CHAPTER 17:

How would you describe what a professional Worship Artist is?

_____

_____

_____

_____

_____

BEFORE READING CHAPTER 18:

Most people can tell you what a Pastor does and what a Worship Leader does, but what does a *Worship Pastor* do?

_____

_____

_____

_____

_____

PART ONE

Foundations of Worship

What Is Worship?

"Worship is our right response to God's revelations."

—STEVEN D. BROOKS

STEVEN BROOKS BEGINS CHAPTER 1 with an important question: "If worshipers are to accomplish the action of worship, shouldn't they first know what the word means?" Although the Bible never provides us with a clear definition of what worship is, it is nevertheless full of snapshots which reveal important aspects of what biblical worship is and is not. Our worship of God here on earth often mirrors how God is worshiped in heaven. The Book of Revelation in particular is a rich resource for this—especially chapters 4 and 5. These biblical descriptions have inspired countless hymns and choruses, and even church architecture.

1. Take time to carefully read through each of the worship definitions in Appendix 1 of your *Worship Quest* book. Quote two (2) definitions (including the author) that you most resonate with and explain why.

_____

_____

_____

_____

_____

_____

_____

2. In this chapter, Brooks addresses the difference between *praise* and *worship*. List two (2) specific acts of *praise* and two (2) specific acts of *worship* that might be used in a congregational worship service. Your answers should be specific and detailed.

_____

_____

_____

_____

_____

_____

_____

3. Brooks also draws attention to four (4) worship related Hebrew and Greek words. List each of these words along with their basic definition, followed by a brief example of how each might be seen in action as part of Christian worship.

_____

_____

_____

_____

_____

_____

_____

_____

MORE TO THINK ABOUT: AUTHENTIC WORSHIP

It has been said that "all that glitters is not gold," and the very same could be said of worship. In today's materialistic and consumer driven culture, many aspects of our Christian faith end up taking on characteristics of the world around us. We live in a culture often marked by overwhelming individualism, where people are encouraged and empowered to shape and define their own understanding of reality. Such thinking infiltrates the church and influences how people worship. When we sing songs and pray prayers, etc. that are self–focused and self–serving, we are often misled in thinking such to be authentic worship. God truly cares about each of us, along with our needs and desires. It is good to bring these before the Lord in prayer. However, we should never neglect the importance of worshiping God for *who he is* and praising him for *what he has done*. Authentic worship lifts him up and extols his name. Authentic worship bows before him in loyal submission and in overwhelming awe. Authentic worship ascribes worth to the Triune God who alone is worthy of it all.

4. Worship is *dialogical*—"a dialogue between God and his people." This dialogue is comprised of both revelation and response. Carefully read Genesis 8:15–20 and explain how it illustrates a dialogical understanding of worship.

_____

_____

_____

_____

_____

_____

_____

_____

Wisdom From The Early Church

"Let our praise be with God, and not of ourselves: for God hateth them that praise themselves."

—CLEMENT OF ROME, FIRST EPISTLE OF CLEMENT

---

5. Since worship is a response to what God has done, is doing, and will do in our lives, reflect on what God has done in *your* life. Briefly summarize something God has done in your life and then quote a Scripture, song, poem, or prayer that might be a good response.

_____

_____

_____

_____

_____

_____

_____

_____

Take A Moment To Pray

Lord, as You guide me by Your Spirit into all truth,
teach me to affirm what it is that makes Christian worship "Christian,"
and what it is that makes Christian worship "worship."
This I pray in the name of the Father and of the Son and of the Holy Spirit. Amen.

MY ACTION PLAN COMMITMENT

Here are the two ways I commit to apply and use what I have learned from chapter 1 in my life and/or ministry setting:

1. _____
   _____

2. _____
   _____

Whom Should We Worship?

"Then I brought your fathers out of Egypt, . . . And you lived in the wilderness a long time. Then I brought you to the land of the Amorites, who lived on the other side of the Jordan. . . . And you went over the Jordan and came to Jericho, and the leaders of Jericho fought against you, and also the Amorites, the Perizzites, the Canaanites, the Hittites, the Girgashites, the Hivites, and the Jebusites. And I gave them into your hand. . . . Now therefore fear the LORD and serve him in sincerity and in faithfulness. Put away the gods that your fathers served beyond the River and in Egypt, and serve the LORD. And if it is evil in your eyes to serve the LORD, choose this day whom you will serve, whether the gods your fathers served in the region beyond the River, or the gods of the Amorites in whose land you dwell. But as for me and my house, we will serve the LORD."

—JOSHUA 24:6–15

1. Name two (2) things people might worship other than the God who created us, along with a possible reason they might do so.

   What? _____

   Possible Reason? _____

   _____

   What? _____

   Possible Reason? _____

   _____

MORE TO THINK ABOUT: CHOOSING TO WORSHIP GOD

As human beings we are all created to worship. This does not necessarily mean we will automatically worship the Triune God who made us, but it's important to note that, by nature, we will all worship some *one* or some *thing*. After living as captives in Egypt for over 400 years (Exod 12:40), and influenced by the worship practices of the nations they later dispossessed, many of God's people ended up either worshiping other gods or were tempted to do so. When God had finished delivering his people out of their captivity and into the promised land, he challenged them to choose whom they would "serve" (the Hebrew word in Joshua 24:15 also means to "worship"). Similarly, each of us have lived under the slavery of sin until Jesus set us free and gave us new life—*our* promised land. We too must choose whom we will worship.

2. Worship that is *Christian* must always be worship of the Triune God. Why is the Trinity such a fundamental Christian belief, and why should worship be involved?

_____

_____

_____

_____

_____

_____

_____

_____

3. Which Scriptures specifically tell us about each of the following, and why?

Worshiping the Father? _____

_____

_____

_____

_____

_____

_____

_____

Worshiping the Son? _____

_____

_____

_____

_____

_____

_____

_____

_____

Worshiping the Holy Spirit? _____

_____

_____

_____

_____

_____

_____

_____

4. Explain the basic interrelationship between each person of the Trinity as it relates to our worship of God.

_____

_____

_____

_____

_____

_____

_____

_____

Wisdom From The Early Church

"Seek God, and not where God lives."

—ABBA SISOES, 4TH/5TH CENTURY

---

5. How does worship that is *Christocentric* "tell the story" of the good news of Jesus Christ?

_____

_____

_____

_____

_____

_____

_____

Take A Moment To Pray

Most merciful God, forgive me

for all the times and all the ways

my devotion to other people and pursuits

have come before You.

Renew within me that life–transforming choice

to serve and worship You

rather than any of the competing "gods" of this world,

and may I model this to others for their good and Your glory.

In Jesus' name,

Amen.

MY ACTION PLAN COMMITMENT

Here are the two ways I commit to apply and use what I have learned from chapter 2 in my life and/or ministry setting:

1. _____

_____

2. _____

_____

CHAPTER 3

Where Should We Worship?

I just want to be where you are,
Dwelling daily in your presence;
I don't want to worship from afar,
Draw me near to where you are.[1]

—DON MOEN

IN THIS CHAPTER, BROOKS guides us through a discovery journey where we learn of the various places God is worshiped in the Scriptures: at the altar, in the tabernacle and temple, throughout the whole earth, and before his throne in heaven.

1. God is omnipresent. What does this mean and why is it important when it comes to worship?

_____

_____

_____

_____

_____

_____

_____

_____

1. "I Want To Be Where You Are" Don Moen © 1989 Integrity's Hosanna! Music; Ninth Avenue Music.

2. What does the Old Testament Tabernacle teach us about worship?

_____

_____

_____

_____

_____

_____

_____

MORE TO THINK ABOUT: TABERNACLE AND TEMPLE

The Tabernacle in the Old Testament not only provides us many insights into the nature of biblical worship, it also helps us better understand the role and ministry of Jesus, who "was tabernacled" among us (the meaning of the Greek verb *skēnoun* in John 1:14). Jesus actually became the tabernacle—the tent of meeting—where humanity and Almighty God meet. This new reality in Jesus also replaced the Temple and the priesthood, with believers in Christ together becoming both a holy temple and a holy priesthood, offering our worship unto God (1 Pet 2:5).

3. From the various Old Testament *altars* that Brooks describes in this chapter, which one (1) most inspires you and why? Cite a Scripture passage that mentions/describes it.

_____

_____

_____

_____

_____

_____

_____

The Psalmist affirms that, *"The heavens declare the glory of God, and the sky above proclaims his handiwork. Their voice goes out through all the earth, and their words to the end of the world"* (Ps 19:1, 4a). We similarly hear at the end of the New Testament, *"And I heard every creature in heaven and on earth and under the earth and in the sea, and all that is in them, saying, 'To him who sits on the throne and to the Lamb be blessing and honor and glory and might forever and ever!'"* (Rev 5:13).

4. Since all of creation worships God, it makes sense that creation itself is naturally a place to offer worship to God. Where in God's creation are you most inclined to worship the Lord, and why?

_____

_____

_____

_____

_____

_____

_____

_____

Wisdom From The Early Church

"Jesus equally condemns the foolishness of all, saying that the worship of both Jews and Samaritans shall be transformed to a truer worship. Jesus in effect says that people will no longer seek after a particular place where God properly dwells. Rather, Jesus is both able to fill and able to contain all things. And so, they shall worship the Lord 'every one from his place' [Zeph 2:11],"

—CYRIL OF ALEXANDRIA, COMMENTARY ON THE GOSPEL OF JOHN 2.4

Take A Moment To Pray

Into Your hands this day:
My rising, my going, my thinking, my praying;
My working, my resting, my earning, my saving;
My worries, my troubles, my dreams, and my plans.
Into Your hands this day, O God.
In the name of the Father, and of the Son, and of the Holy Spirit.

Amen.

MY ACTION PLAN COMMITMENT

Here are the two ways I commit to apply and use what I have learned from chapter 3 in my life and/or ministry setting:

1. _____

_____

2. _____

_____

Why Worship?

*"But if Jesus is to be the lens through which you glimpse the beauty of God, you will discover
what it means to worship, because you will discover what it means to be loved."*[1]

—N. T. WRIGHT

KNOWING *WHAT* WORSHIP IS—BEING able to define it, describe it, and even participate in it—is no guarantee that we will actually *want* to worship. The decision to worship God is just that, a *decision*, and our choosing to worship God will be affected by our coming to terms with *why* we should worship him.

1. In chapter 4, Brooks takes a good deal of time explaining the various reasons *why* we should worship God. Explain *why* each of the following reasons is important (cite Scripture where you can) and describe *how significant* it has been in your own worship experience.

   Because Worship Is What We Were Created For

   _____

   _____

   _____

   _____

   _____

   _____

   _____

   _____

1. Wright, *For All God's Worth: True Worship and the Calling of the Church*, 10.

Because Worship Rehearses God's Story

_____

_____

_____

_____

_____

_____

_____

_____

Because Worship Celebrates God

_____

_____

_____

_____

_____

_____

_____

_____

Because Worship Joins/Is Part Of An Eternal Effort

_____

_____

_____

_____

_____

_____

_____

_____

Because Worship Forms Us Spiritually

_____

_____

_____

_____

_____

_____

_____

_____

Because Jesus Tells Us To Worship

_____

_____

_____

_____

_____

_____

_____

_____

2. In this chapter, Brooks summarizes eight specific ways worship forms us spiritually. Which of these has most impacted your own spiritual development and why? Which has had the least impact and why?

_____

_____

_____

_____

_____

_____

_____

_____

3. How is the worship of God impacted when the worship services of a congregation are conducted to attract "seekers" who do not yet know Christ?

_____

_____

_____

_____

_____

_____

_____

_____

_____

MORE TO THINK ABOUT:
WHEN SALVATION IS VIEWED AS A TRANSACTION

Having a personal relationship with Christ is a vital part of the Christian faith. As important as this relationship is, our salvation was never meant to only be a once–for–all–time decision (i.e. a *transaction*), but more like a journey—a journey to be pursued within a community of faith. When salvation and conversion are viewed as a transaction, many people end up defending their "personal relationship with Christ" as a reason for no longer needing to be part of a worshiping community. Because salvation is a process and not merely a transaction, the Apostle Paul urged believers in Philippians 2:12 to *"work out your salvation with fear and trembling"* (the word "your" is actually plural). We are meant to work out our salvation *together* (see chapter 8 on Corporate Worship for more).

---

4. Brooks draws attention to how doing things *for* God might actually prevent people from deeply knowing God themselves. He then quotes Robert Mulholland as saying, "They were so busy *being in the world for God* that they failed to *be in God for the world*." What is a specific example of how you've seen this danger at work?

_____

_____

_____

_____

_____

_____

_____

_____

Wisdom From The Early Church

"O Lord our God, who has bidden the light to shine out of darkness, who has again wakened us to praise your goodness and ask for your grace; accept now, in your endless mercy, the sacrifice of our worship and thanksgiving, and grant unto us all such requests as may be wholesome for us."

—GREEK CHURCH LITURGY, 2ND CENTURY

Take A Moment To Pray

Grace us, O God,
with hearts that trust, minds that yield, and hands that serve.
Grace us, O God,
with strength that lasts, hope that waits, and joy that heals.
Grace us, O God,
This day and every day.
In Jesus' name,
Amen.

MY ACTION PLAN COMMITMENT

Here are the two ways I commit to use and apply what I have learned from chapter 4 in my life and/or ministry setting:

1. _____
   _____

2. _____
   _____

CHAPTER 5

Who Is Welcome to Worship?

And they devoted themselves to the apostles' teaching and the fellowship, to the breaking of bread and the prayers. . . . And day by day, attending the temple together and breaking bread in their homes, they received their food with glad and generous hearts, praising God and having favor with all the people. And the Lord added to their number day by day those who were being saved.

—ACTS 2:42–47

JESUS MODELED AN EXTRAORDINARY level of love and compassion for people from every corner of society: Gentiles and Jews, the poor and the rich, zealots and doubters, religious hypocrites and devoted disciples, the despised and the respected. He was often criticized for his radical practices of inclusion:

> *And as Jesus reclined at table in the house, behold, many tax collectors and sinners came and were reclining with Jesus and his disciples. And when the Pharisees saw this, they said to his disciples, "Why does your teacher eat with tax collectors and sinners?" But when he heard it, he said, "Those who are well have no need of a physician, but those who are sick. Go and learn what this means: 'I desire mercy, and not sacrifice.' For I came not to call the righteous, but sinners." (Matt 9:10–13)*

> *So he came to a town in Samaria called Sychar, near the plot of ground Jacob had given to his son Joseph. Jacob's well was there, and Jesus, tired as he was from the journey, sat down by the well. It was about the sixth hour. When a Samaritan woman came to draw water, Jesus said to her, "Will you give me a drink?" (His disciples had gone into the town to buy food.) The Samaritan woman said to him, "You are a Jew and I am a Samaritan woman. How can you ask me for a drink?" (For Jews do not associate with Samaritans.) Jesus answered her, "If you knew the gift of God and who it is that asks you for a drink, you would have asked him and he would have given you living water." (John 4:5–10, NIV)*

1. The above passages further illustrate what Brooks has drawn attention to—the worship given to Jesus by a woman assumed to be a prostitute (Luke 7:36–39, 44–50). Carefully reread each of these passages. If Jesus were living in our world today, who might people be shocked to find him associating with or accepting worship from?

_____

_____

_____

_____

_____

_____

_____

MORE TO THINK ABOUT:
LOVE FOR THE STRANGER

The Apostle Paul urged the Christians in Rome, *"Contribute to the needs of the saints and seek to show hospitality"* (Rom 12:13), and the writer of Hebrews exhorted believers, "Do not neglect to show hospitality to strangers, for thereby some have entertained angels unawares (Heb 13:2)." In these and other New Testament passages, the word for "hospitality" is the Greek word *philoxenos*—literally meaning, "love for the stranger." Early Celtic missionaries would actually invite pagan "strangers" to join them in their worship of God and service to the community. In time, these "strangers" regularly came to believe in Christ themselves!

---

2. Reread the "call to worship" by Jim Altizer cited at the end of chapter 5, then make a list of people in your own city and community who might be a challenge for people to worship alongside.

_____

_____

_____

_____

_____

_____

_____

3. What other expectations or "barriers" do you think might prevent people from feeling comfortable and welcomed at the worship services of many churches today?

_____

_____

_____

_____

_____

_____

_____

_____

Wisdom From The Early Church

"Every day they continued to meet together ... praising God and enjoying the favor of all the people. And the Lord added to their number daily those who were being saved."

—ACTS 2:46–47 (NIV, EMPHASIS ADDED)

After describing the difficult life–struggles of hymn writer William Cowper and then of King David in 2 Samuel, Brooks concludes that "When you are in times of deep struggle, the only thing you can do that has any substance or value at all, is to worship!" Whether or not they realize it, worshiping God is exactly what every person needs, regardless of who they are or what others may think of them.

4. Describe a difficult time you had to go through in your life. If you chose to worship God in the midst of it all, describe how you did this and how it made you feel. If you did not worship God at that time in your life, describe how things may have been different had you done so.

_____

_____

_____

_____

_____

_____

_____

_____

Take A Moment To Pray

O Father, You who love all people perfectly;

Forgive me for distancing myself

from those who dress differently, talk differently, or act differently than me.

Do a work in me, so that without hesitation,

I will wholeheartedly worship You alongside any who might be a stranger to me.

Help me to welcome all, even as You welcome all to put their trust in You.

This I pray through Your Son, Jesus Christ.

Amen.

MY ACTION PLAN COMMITMENT

Here are the two ways I commit to use and apply what I have learned from chapter 5 in my life and/or ministry setting:

1. _____

_____

2. _____

_____

CHAPTER 6

How Should We Worship?

"And David danced before the LORD with all his might."

—2 SAMUEL 6:14A

SADLY, MUCH OF WHAT passes for worship today is rather anemic, even though we are repeatedly reminded to love God with all our heart, soul, mind, and strength (Mark 12:30). Brooks reminds us that worship must originate in our *hearts* but then be expressed in our *actions*. One without the other will become either passive or empty ritual.

1. Biblical worship is expressed with both our heart and our action. In your own words, describe what worship might look like that is full of heart, but no real action. Then describe what worship might look like that is all action, but with little to no heart involved.

_____

_____

_____

_____

_____

_____

_____

2. Bowing, kneeling, and prostration are widely practiced in the worship of God throughout both Old and New Testaments. Why do you believe it to be so common? What two (2) examples of this practice that Brooks mentions from Scripture should motivate us to do likewise and why?

_____

_____

_____

_____

_____

_____

_____

3. Are worship related rituals inherently a bad thing? Why or why not?

_____

_____

_____

_____

_____

_____

_____

_____

MORE TO THINK ABOUT:
THE SACRIFICE OF PRAISE

One of the early praise choruses I remember singing back in the 1980's was Kirk Dearman's "We Bring the Sacrifice of Praise." But what exactly should a sacrifice of praise look like? In part, the writer of Hebrews provides an answer: "Through Jesus, therefore, let us continually offer to God a **sacrifice** of praise—the fruit of lips that openly profess his name. And do not forget to do good and to share with others, for with such **sacrifices** God is pleased" (Heb 13:15–16, NIV, emphasis added). In both instances, the original Greek word for sacrifice is *thusia*, suggesting that our sacrifice of praise to God is not only to be on our lips, but is also to be in the goodness and generosity we extend to others.

4. Brooks stresses that some people "struggle with the ideas of guidelines for worship because we live in a culture that emphasizes fluid responsibility." Is flexibility and change a good thing when it comes to Christian worship? Why or why not?

_____

_____

_____

_____

_____

_____

_____

_____

Wisdom From The Early Church

"In the beginning there is struggle and a lot of work for those who come near to God. But after that there is indescribable joy . . . Thus we ought to light the divine fire in ourselves with tears and effort."

—AMMA SYNCLETICA OF ALEXANDRIA, 3RD CENTURY

Take A Moment To Pray

All–Powerful and Inescapable One,

capture and overtake us this day:

Bind our hearts with security;

Shackle our souls with resiliency;

Overwhelm our minds with mystery.

Capture and overtake us this day, O God.

In the name of the Father, and of the Son, and of the Holy Spirit.

Amen.

MY ACTION PLAN COMMITMENT

Here are the two ways I commit to use and apply what I have learned from chapter 6 in my life and/or ministry setting:

1. _____
   _____

2. _____
   _____

PART TWO

Practices of Worship

CHAPTER 7

Personal Worship

> I will come and bow down
> At Your feet, Lord Jesus.
> In Your presence is fullness of joy.
> There is nothing, there is no one
> Who compares with You.
> I take pleasure in worshiping You Lord.[1]
>
> —MARTY NYSTROM

BEFORE ONE CAN EFFECTIVELY lead others in worshiping God, one must be a worshiper themself. A true leader should always lead by example. How is it possible to lead others in a personal encounter with Almighty God through worship, if you have not made it a regular part of your own life and practice? This is why the Apostle Paul urged the Philippian believers: *"Dear brothers and sisters, pattern your lives after mine, and learn from those who follow our example"* (Phil 3:17). Our example as a worshiper must naturally flow out of our own genuine love for God. As Brooks emphasizes, "Our personal worship plants our hearts deep in the love of God so that we might know how wide, long, high and deep his love for us truly is. . . . When we realize just how abundant God's love for us is, how can we not respond in worship and praise?"

---

1. "I Will Come and Bow Down" Martin Nystrom © 1984 Integrity's Hosanna! Music.

1. Take a moment to think about how God is the One who actually initiates our worship of him. Describe how *you* have experienced this to be true in your life?

_____

_____

_____

_____

_____

_____

_____

2. One of the primary ways God initiates our worship of him is by means of his great love for us. Brooks draws attention to this by including the lyrics to the great hymn by Frederick Lehman entitled "The Love of God." Carefully reread the hymn's lyrics, then write down two (2) of its lines that resonate the most with you and explain why.

_____

_____

_____

_____

_____

_____

_____

3. Take some time to carefully read Hebrews 12:28–29. According to this passage, what should our motivation be for worshiping God? What might God be saying to you from these verses?

_____

_____

_____

_____

_____

_____

_____

4. There are times when we may not *feel* like worshiping the Lord. It seems that David experienced this as well, actually commanding himself to bless the Lord. Read Psalm 103 and note how many times this idea is repeated. Why does David seem to consider this so important? Why might this be a good and helpful practice for us as well?

_____

_____

_____

_____

_____

_____

_____

_____

MORE TO THINK ABOUT:
THE INTEGRITY OF PERSONAL WORSHIP

The commitment a worship leader makes to deepen their own personal worship of God is important. In part, such a commitment demonstrates a leader's desire to worship God whether or not anyone else around them does. There may be times when you are leading worship with all your heart, soul, mind, and strength, and it feels like you're the only one doing so. In such a case, do you stop? No! Your commitment to worship God no matter what, is a powerful statement that God deserves to be worshiped at all times and in all places. A decision to personally and confidently worship God even when others don't seem interested is a matter of integrity. If you haven't already done so, make a decision to be as committed to worshiping the Lord when you're alone as you are when you're with others.

"For we aim at what is honorable not only in the Lord's sight but also in the sight of man" (2 Cor 8:21).

5. What might help you to set aside more *alone time* with God, and why is this important for you to grow as a worshiper?

_____

_____

_____

_____

_____

_____

_____

_____

6. As humans, we naturally worship something. Brooks uses a helpful quote by Harold Best to reinforce an important question: "Who or what are you worshiping?" If you were to be completely honest, describe *someone* or *something* that may have captured your affections too much and put you at risk of worshiping wrongly.

_____

_____

_____

_____

_____

_____

_____

Wisdom From The Early Church

"They appear to me a mirror of the soul of every one who sings them; they enable him to perceive his own emotions, and to express them in the words of the Psalms. He who hears them read receives them as if they were spoken for him. Conscience–struck, he will either humbly repent, or hearing how the trust of believers was rewarded by God, rejoice as if His mercy were promised to him in particular, and begin to thank God. Yet, in its pages you find portrayed man's whole life, the emotion of his soul, and the frames of his mind. We cannot conceive of anything richer than the Book of Psalms. If you need penitence, if anguish or temptation have befallen you, if you have escaped persecution and oppression, or are immersed in deep affliction, concerning each and all you may find instruction, and state it to God in the words of the Psalter!"

—ATHANASIUS (C. 296–373) BISHOP OF ALEXANDRIA

Take A Moment To Pray

May we worship and bow down.
Before You, King of Glory;
May we all cast down our crowns;
May we lay our lives before You,
for You are Lord of all.
Amen.

MY ACTION PLAN COMMITMENT

Here are the two ways I commit to use and apply what I have learned from chapter 7 in my life and/or ministry setting:

1. _____

   _____

2. _____

   _____

Corporate Worship

". . . Christianity is essentially a social religion;
and that to turn it into a solitary religion, is indeed to destroy it."

—JOHN WESLEY,
UPON OUR LORD'S SERMON ON THE MOUNT

AS IMPORTANT AS PERSONAL worship is, we were not created to only worship God privately. God created us to worship him in community.

1. In chapter 8, Brooks makes an interesting assertion: "What many people consider corporate worship is actually personal worship happening in a corporate setting." What is it about *corporate worship* that truly makes it *corporate*?

_____

_____

_____

_____

_____

_____

_____

_____

2. Explain the difference between "vertical worship" and "horizontal worship" and why both are necessary.

_____

_____

_____

_____

_____

_____

_____

_____

3. What is it within the lengthy quote by Alexander Schmemann in this chapter that got you thinking about corporate worship differently and why?

_____

_____

_____

_____

_____

_____

_____

_____

_____

MORE TO THINK ABOUT:
THE WORK OF THE PEOPLE

The Greek word, _leitourgia_ (introduced in chapter 1), is often translated, "the work of the people." Worship is not meant to solely be the work of _a person_, but rather the work of _the people_. When people gather together for corporate times of worship, they are always meant to be participants, not spectators. Corporate responsibility for worship should be shared. This is why the Apostle Paul tells the church in Corinth:

> _"Well, my brothers and sisters, let's summarize. When you meet together, one will sing, another will teach, another will tell some special revelation God has given, one will speak in tongues, and another will interpret what is said. But everything that is done must strengthen all of you."_ (1 Cor 14:26, NLT)

Corporate worship times should be characterized by a wide variety of participation, with people singing, reading Scripture, praying, playing an instrument, serving the Lord's Supper, and participating in worship related dance, drama, etc. It is biblical and a glory to God when our worship is the _work of the people!_

Wisdom From The Early Church

*"Let us, too, lift up our voices by singing or praying in church, so that our adversary,
the devil, may depart in confusion at the holy sound."*

—*CAESARIUS OF ARLES, SERMON 80.2*

Take A Moment To Pray

O Lord,

You who desire table fellowship with us,

inspire us to desire table fellowship with others:

Family members, Christ followers, strangers, and neighbors.

May we invite You to work in us and through us,

as we yield to Your reign,

always seating You at the head of our table.

In the name of the Father, and of the Son, and of the Holy Spirit.

Amen.

MY ACTION PLAN COMMITMENT

Here are the two ways I commit to use and apply what I have learned from chapter 8 in my life and/or ministry setting:

1. _____
   _____

2. _____
   _____

CHAPTER **9**

Lifestyle Worship

"In our personal times of devotion or in the middle of public praise services, the God of the entire universe is our fascinated audience. He does not check to see if we are singing on pitch. He does not check to see if we are on the worship team. Over and over there is a cry from heaven of 'Let me hear your voice.' He wants to hear our sound. He longs to hear our voices: 'My dove in the clefts of the rock, in the hiding places on the mountainside, show me your face, let me hear your voice, for your voice is sweet, and your face is lovely' (Song of Solomon 3:14)."[1]

—JULIE MEYER

WORSHIP THAT IS BIBLICAL and heartfelt is inherently transforming. Jesus made it clear that the Father was seeking true worshipers who worship in spirit and in truth. To be a worshiper in truth is to be a worshiper in reality—and one's life is meant to be a reflection of this. As we worship God in this way, we should expect to grow in the ways of God and reflect his character and heart.

1. Reread the two quotes by Mark Labberton in chapter 9. Why is the connection between worship and justice such an important one for worshipers to embrace, and what should this look like in the lives of believers today?

----

1. Meyer, *Singing the Scriptures*, 74.

2. In the Old Testament, the prophet Micah declares, *"He has showed you, O man, what is good. And what does the LORD require of you? To act justly and to love mercy and to walk humbly with your God"* (Mic 6:8, NIV). Justice. Mercy. Humility. Why do you think *all three* of these are needed?

_____

_____

_____

_____

_____

_____

_____

_____

Wisdom From The Early Church

"You ask what you should offer: offer yourself. For what else does the Lord seek of you but you? Because of all earthly creatures he has made nothing better than you, he seeks yourself from yourself, because you have lost yourself."

—AUGUSTINE, SERMON 48.2

---

3. In the New Testament, the Apostle Paul writes, *"Or do you not know that your body is the temple of the Holy Spirit who is in you, whom you have from God, and you are not your own? For you were bought at a price. Therefore glorify God with your body"* (1 Cor 6:19–20, NET). What is it about Paul's words that might be offensive to people in today's world? What might the benefits be to living out these words in our lives?

_____

_____

_____

_____

_____

_____

_____

_____

MORE TO THINK ABOUT:
SACRIFICIAL LIVING

Biblical worship involves much, much more than singing songs to God. The Apostle Paul reminds us of this: *"And so, dear brothers and sisters, I plead with you to give your bodies to God because of all he has done for you. Let them be a living and holy sacrifice—the kind he will find acceptable. This is truly the way to worship him"* (Rom 12:1, NLT).

Take A Moment To Pray

Your word on my mind,

Your grace on my lips,

Your love in my heart;

This day and every day, O Lord.

Amen.

MY ACTION PLAN COMMITMENT

Here are the two ways I commit to use and apply what I have learned from chapter 9 in my life and/or ministry setting:

1. _____

_____

2. _____

_____

PART THREE

Gatherings of Worship

CHAPTER 10

The Private Worship Gathering

It is a difficult lesson to learn today,
to leave one's friends and family and
deliberately practice the art of solitude
for an hour or a day or a week.
For me, the break is most difficult . . .

And yet, once done,
I find there a quality to being alone
that is incredibly precious.
Life rushes back into the void,
richer, more vivid, fuller than before![1]

—ANNE MORROW LINDBERG

1. Describe how your private times of worshiping God are different than when you're worshiping with others.

_____

_____

_____

_____

_____

_____

_____

_____

1. Lindberg, *Celtic Daily Prayer, Book One*, 27.

2. In Psalm 46, the Lord declares, *"Be still, and know that I am God"* (Ps 46:10a). Why do you suppose practicing stillness during worship is so difficult for most people? What might help us to overcome this difficulty?

_____

_____

_____

_____

_____

_____

_____

Wisdom From The Early Church

It was said of Abba John that when he returned from the harvest of when he had been with some of the old men, he gave himself to prayer, meditation and psalmody until his thoughts were re–established in their previous order.

—*ABBA JOHN THE DWARF, 4TH CENTURY*

MORE TO THINK ABOUT:
GET AWAY FOR A PRIVATE PRAYER & WORSHIP RETREAT

Times of private worship can certainly take place during your morning "quiet times," daily devotions, or during a variety of ordinary activities. However, it is also important for those involved in worship leadership to set aside exclusive times for worshiping the Lord through song, prayer, Scripture reading, silent listening, and reflection. Getting away from the normal routines of life and ministry in order to spend exclusive time with the Lord is often referred to as a "prayer retreat." Such times can be powerfully transformative in one's life and ministry.

"To intentionally place oneself in God's presence and to ask, Lord, what do you think of me? Lord, what changes do you desire in my life and ministry? To have these questions in mind as one reflects on the Scriptures, covenants made, the writing of the saints, and the events of our time is to provide opportunity for the Lord to draw us toward greater faithfulness" (Rueben P. Job and Norman Shawchuck, *A Guide to Prayer for Ministers and Other Servants*, 12).

There is little that can deepen and strengthen the life of a worshiper or worship leader than taking a personal prayer retreat!

3. Spending time reading God's word is a wonderful way to promote the personal and private worship of God in your life. How we go about reading Scripture, however, is just as important and impacting as the Scriptures are themselves. In Appendix 4, Brooks introduces readers to the ancient spiritual practice of *Lectio Divina* (divine reading). Select one of the following Scripture passages and then slowly work through the five steps described in Appendix 4. Use the space below to record your thoughts and discoveries as this spiritual discipline helps you encounter your chosen text in a deeper way.

Choose one: **Psalm 23:1–6; Matthew 14:26–33; Romans 1:21–22, 25; 1 Peter 5:5b–7**

Step 1 (*Lectio*): What text did you select, and how long did you allow yourself to read, reread, and "soak" in the text?

_____

_____

_____

_____

_____

_____

_____

Step 2 (*Meditatio*): Assuming this text is personally addressed to you, what specific things was the Lord wanting to say to you?

_____

_____

_____

_____

_____

_____

_____

Step 3 (*Oratio*): Take the things you sense God is wanting you to hear from this text, and in your own words write a prayer, asking God to help you accomplish these very things in your life.

_____

_____

_____

_____

_____

_____

_____

Step 4 (*Contemplatio*): In silence, ponder how your encounter with God and his Word has changed or will change you. Take time to "soak" (and be still) in this new reality. Afterward, describe what this entire *Lectio Divina* experience was like for you (if you are working though this Workbook as a group, write down your experience and then share it with the group):

_____

_____

_____

_____

_____

_____

_____

_____

Take A Moment To Pray

May I go forth and declare my love for You,

with pledge and prayer and songs of praise;

With justice and mercy that honor Your Name;

With thoughts and words and attitudes and deeds;

May I go forth and declare my love for You, O Lord,

this day and every day.

Amen.

MY ACTION PLAN COMMITMENT

Here are the two ways I commit to use and apply what I have learned from chapter 10 in my life and/or ministry setting:

1. _____

_____

2. _____

_____

CHAPTER 11

The Family Worship Gathering

"There are no 'silver bullets' or 'golden hamsters' that can stay all the monsters threatening humanity at this moment in time. But if we did just one thing, this one thing would dramatically change, for the better, the world in which we live. The one thing is this: bring back the table. Make the table the most sacred object of furniture in every home, in every church, in every community."

—LEONARD SWEET

BROOKS SUGGESTS THAT "FAMILY Worship occurs when small group gatherings, made up of people who are familiar to one another, worship together." This could be a small group, a home group, a cell group, a life group, a prayer group, a Bible study group, or some other such group. Worship often occurs in such gatherings whether or not it is part of the group's stated purpose, and when it does, the value of worshiping together deepens that group's relationship with the Lord and one another. The Christian faith is meant to be a "one another" faith. In the New Testament, the Greek word *allēlōn*, translated "one another," is used 100 times, making it quite clear we are meant to live out our faith in ways that include and benefit others. Small group "family" worship should be the practice of all Christ followers.

1. Select two (2) from the following list of "one another" Scriptures you consider to be the most important in the life of a small group. Write two (2) or three (3) sentences regarding each of your two Scriptures, explaining why you believe them to be the most important.

Mark 9:50	John 13:34–35	Romans 15:14
1 Corinthians 12:25	2 Corinthians 13:11	Galatians 5:13
Ephesians 4:32	Colossians 3:16	1 Thessalonians 5:11
Hebrews 10:24	James 5:16	1 Peter 5:5

    _____
    _____
    _____
    _____
    _____
    _____
    _____
    _____
    _____
    _____
    _____
    _____
    _____
    _____
    _____
    _____
    _____

2. Think about your own ordinary weekly routines. How might you facilitate spontaneous *opportunities* to worship with friends, family, coworkers, or others? Describe two (2) such opportunities.

    _____
    _____
    _____
    _____
    _____
    _____
    _____
    _____

3. The early churches that the Apostle Paul established were generally small "house churches," meeting in people's private homes. They would have been similar to the small, "family" gatherings Brooks describes in chapter 11. With this in mind, read Colossians 3:12–17, and imagine these instructions were given today to you and the small group of believers you are part of. How should these words impact how you and your group worship the Lord?

_____

_____

_____

_____

_____

_____

_____

_____

_____

Wisdom From The Early Church

"O good Shepherd, seek me out, and bring me home to your fold again. Deal favorably with me according to your good pleasure, that I may dwell in your house all the days of my life, and praise you for ever and ever with them that are there."
—ST. JEROME, 4TH/5TH CENTURY

MORE TO THINK ABOUT:
THE LORD'S SUPPER IN SMALL GROUP MEETINGS

The quote by Leonard Sweet at the beginning of this Workbook chapter may have been a bit puzzling, unless you recognize the historical and theological connection between common meals we share together and the eucharistic meal that Jesus instituted and instructed his followers to regularly observe. In the earliest churches, the Lord's Supper was integrated into a common meal that believers shared together (read 1 Corinthians 11). Over time, the Lord's Supper became a distinct, sacramental meal. The fact remains, however, that house churches in the first and even second century observed the importance of *the table*—sharing meals and the Lord's Supper together on a regular (at least weekly) basis. When it comes to times of family/small group worship today, observing the Lord's Supper together may be more beneficial than you'd imagine.

4. In what ways, either for good or bad, might people's "personal worship" affect the small group "family worship" discussed in chapter 11?

_____

_____

_____

_____

_____

_____

_____

Take A Moment To Pray

O Lord, guide us into all truth—
The truth about others and the truth about ourselves.
Grant us Your wisdom to see beyond our shortsightedness
and our preoccupations.
Then gird us with Your peace—
The peace that accepts; and trusts; and rests;
In the name of the Father, and of the Son, and of the Holy Spirit.
Amen.

MY ACTION PLAN COMMITMENT

Here are the two ways I commit to use and apply what I have learned from chapter 11 in my life and/or ministry setting:

1. _____

   _____

2. _____

   _____

The Congregational Worship Gathering

"Gathered worship offers us an opportunity to practice classic Christian disciplines such as prayer, Bible reading, worship, and confession alongside fellow Christians. Church services, therefore, are habit–forming in that they help us form and maintain essential practices and rhythms that contribute to a vibrant walk with the Lord."[1]

—RORY NOLAND

1. In what ways are ethnicity and culture often the same when it comes to musical worship, and in what ways are they sometimes different?

_____

_____

_____

_____

_____

_____

_____

_____

1. Noland, *Transforming Worship*, 68.

2. In chapter 12, Brooks asserts that, despite the opinion of some, musical worship in particular is absolutely a matter of "style." Since the church is by nature multi-cultural and multi-ethnic, why is *convergence worship* a wise and effective practice for congregational worship?

_____

_____

_____

_____

_____

_____

_____

3. Explain what makes *convergence worship* different from *blended worship*, then describe what the difference between them might look like in a worship gathering. Be specific.

_____

_____

_____

_____

_____

_____

_____

_____

MORE TO THINK ABOUT:
WE NEED EVERYONE

It is relatively easy to categorize people within a church's worship service: singers and non-singers, worship team members and congregants, clergy and laity. An inherent danger in categorizing people is that we might be tempted to consider some categories as more important in worship than others. Apparently, the believers in ancient Corinth struggled with this very thing. In response, the Apostle Paul reminded them, *"For the body does not consist of one member but of many. . . . If the whole body were an eye, where would be the sense of hearing? If the whole body were an ear, where would be the sense of smell? . . . As it is, there are many parts, yet one body"* (1 Cor 12:14–20).

4. Carefully reread the footnote "Tips for planning a convergent worship service," as well as Appendix 3 (*Convergence Worship :: Old, New, Borrowed, Blue*). Using Brooks' guidelines, sketch out what an entire congregational worship service should look like, centered around 1 Peter 1:15–16, *"but as he who called you is holy, you also be holy in all your conduct, since it is written, 'You shall be holy, for I am holy.'"* Cite specific songs, readings, prayers, and other acts of worship in your convergent worship service plan. If you are unfamiliar with planning an entire worship service, Appendix 7 might be of help.

_____

_____

_____

_____

_____

_____

_____

_____

Wisdom From The Early Church

"As this piece of bread was scattered over the hills and then was brought together and made one, so let your church be brought together from the ends of the earth into your kingdom. For yours is the glory and the power through Jesus Christ forever."

—DIDACHE, LATE 1ST CENTURY

---

5. In what specific ways does the convergent worship service you planned above take into account the multiple ethnicities and generations found within the body of Christ? If it doesn't, then what changes could you make in order for it to do so?

_____

_____

_____

_____

_____

_____

_____

_____

Take A Moment To Pray

Do a mighty work in Your people;

Draw near to us, O Mighty One;

Stay close to us, O Loving One;

Soak in to us, O Holy One.

Do a mighty work in Your people;

This day and every day, O Lord.

Amen.

MY ACTION PLAN COMMITMENT

Here are the two ways I commit to use and apply what I have learned from chapter 12 in my life and/or ministry setting:

1. _____

_____

2. _____

_____

CHAPTER 13

The Festival Worship Gathering

"Worship is transformative when it effects personal change and elicits practical response. This sense of transformation is imparted to participants by providing resources for living a 'worship lifestyle' long after the concert is over."[1]

—MONIQUE M. INGALLS

1. Brooks points out that "the primary purpose of the festival gathering is to encourage personal and lifestyle worship." How is Festival Worship inherently different than Congregational Worship?

_____

_____

_____

_____

_____

_____

_____

_____

1. Ingalls, *Singing the Congregation*, 63–64.

2. Describe your past experience(s) attending a Festival Worship Gathering. How did it make you feel and how did it impact your relationship with God? If you have not attended such an event, what have you learned from the experiences of people you know who have attended?

_____

_____

_____

_____

_____

_____

_____

_____

3. What advantages might festival worship have over other types of worship gatherings, especially congregational worship? What advantages might congregational worship have over festival worship?

_____

_____

_____

_____

_____

_____

_____

_____

MORE TO THINK ABOUT: STADIUM WORSHIP

If Scripture affirms, *"It is true that some preach Christ out of envy and rivalry, but others out of goodwill. But what does it matter? The important thing is that in every way, whether from false motives or true, Christ is preached. And because of this I rejoice"* (Phil 1:15, 18, NIV), then shouldn't the same principle apply to the worship of God? Worship scholar, Monique Ingalls seems to think so.

"In order to be 'authentic worship,' the worship concert must be experienced as a participatory performance, in which the boundary between the worship leader at center stage and the audience in the stadium seats is collapsed because both are engaged in the act of worship. Attendees must understand both themselves and the worship leaders onstage as 'worshipers'—equal participants in the activity of worship."—Monique M. Ingalls, *Singing the Congregation: How Contemporary Worship Music Forms Evangelical Community*, 56.

You might be among those who consider "worship concerts" held in stadiums to be somewhat suspect, but if the Lord is truly being worshiped there, perhaps we shouldn't be so quick to criticize.

Wisdom From The Early Church

"Those of you who are healthy, thank him for it; those of you that are sick, run to him to be healed. All of you, say, 'Come, let us worship and prostrate ourselves before him, and let us weep before the Lord who made us,' made us human beings and saved us.'"

—AUGUSTINE, SERMON 176.5

Take A Moment To Pray

Gracious God,
through every means possible,
shape me into someone who worships You
with all my heart, soul, mind, and strength.
Deepen within me the desire to worship You
wherever I go and whoever I'm with,
and help me to gain as much as I can
from being with other worshipers.
Through Christ and Christ alone I pray.

Amen.

MY ACTION PLAN COMMITMENT

Here are the two ways I commit to use and apply what I have learned from chapter 13 in my life and/or ministry setting:

1. _____
   _____

2. _____
   _____

PART FOUR

Roles of Worship Leadership

CHAPTER 14

The Call of Worship Leadership

"God doesn't call the qualified. He qualifies the called."

—BILLY GRAHAM

1. What is it about worshiping God and helping others to worship God that most excites you?

_____

_____

_____

_____

_____

_____

_____

_____

2. When you think about leading others in worship, what Scripture verse or passage comes to mind and why?

_____

_____

_____

_____

_____

_____

_____

_____

Whether you have experienced a *dramatic* call, a *prolonged call*, or what Brooks terms a *realized call*, the very fact you are here reading the book, *Worship Quest*, and making your way through this Workbook, likely indicates that you have been called by God to worship leadership in some capacity (If you are using this Workbook as a group study and have not been called to serve in worship leadership within the church, you can skip this question. I would, however, encourage you to ask the worship leader in your church about his or her calling to worship leadership).

3. Of the three specific types of calls listed above (from chapter 14), which best describes your call into worship leadership? Why do you believe this to be the case? If you are unsure, and had to choose, which one "might" be unfolding in your life and why?

_____
_____
_____
_____
_____
_____
_____
_____

MORE TO THINK ABOUT:
WHEN YOU'RE STRUGGLING WITH SELF-DOUBT

At one time or another, nearly everyone God has called into Christian ministry will struggle with self-doubt and suspect that their calling is no longer valid. When this happens, recall what the Apostle Paul reminds the Roman believers: *"For God's gifts and his call can never be withdrawn"* (Rom 11:29, NLT). God hasn't changed his mind about you or taken away your gifting! You may have made mistakes or gone through some tough times, but God still believes in you. His gifts and calling in your life are there to stay!

Wisdom From The Early Church

"We are the true worshipers and the true priests: praying in the spirit, we make our sacrifice of prayer in spirit, and offering which is God's own and acceptable to him. . . . This is the sacrifice, offered from the heart, fed on faith, prepared by truth; unblemished in innocence, pure in chastity, garlanded with love, which we must bring to God's altar, in a procession of good works, to the accompaniment of psalms and hymns. It will obtain for us from God all that we ask."

—TERTULLIAN, ON PRAYER, 28–29

Take A Moment To Pray

Save us, O Lord:

From the worries that trouble us,

and the troubles that worry us;

From the challenges that burden us,

and the burdens that challenge us;

Save us, O Lord:

From the doubts that hinder us,

the fears that cripple us,

and the failures that haunt us;

Save us, O Lord this day and every day.

In the name of the Father, and of the Son, and of the Holy Spirit.

Amen.

MY ACTION PLAN COMMITMENT

Here are the two ways I commit to use and apply what I have learned from chapter 14 in my life and/or ministry setting:

1. _____
   _____

2. _____
   _____

CHAPTER 15

Worship Leader

"Piety cannot be granted or inherited; it must be cultivated. For Worship Leaders, this means that one must be devoted to growing and maintaining an ongoing, secret relationship with God above all else: above finding the right song; above the quality of the music; and above the honing of his or her musical gifts. The continual, disciplined renewal of this secret life with Christ is priority number one, and there is no shortcut or substitute."[1]

—*JIM ALTIZER*

Of the four worship leadership "roles" that Brooks discusses in chapters 15–18, *worship leader* is the most commonly used title in churches today. The widespread use of *worship leader* does not mean, however, that the title is always used properly. It is not uncommon for church volunteers and leaders who are in front of God's people "leading worship," to in fact be something other than a true worship leader. This doesn't minimize or trivialize the importance of their role or their contribution to the worship ministry of the church. It is nevertheless helpful to understand, then, what truly makes a "worship leader" a Worship Leader.

1. As an illustration of what should characterize a true Worship Leader, Brooks uses two analogies—the first of a tour guide and the second of the Palm Sunday donkey. What is it about these analogies that strikes you as being essential for anyone called to be a Worship Leader? Explain your answer and provide two (2) Scripture verses in support.

_____

_____

_____

_____

_____

_____

_____

_____

1. Altizer, *The Making of a Worship Leader*, 77.

2. In John 3:30, John the Baptist declares, concerning Jesus, *"He must increase but I must decrease."* Describe two (2) specific ways you think a Worship Leader should apply John's declaration to their own worship leading ministry.

_____

_____

_____

_____

_____

_____

_____

_____

3. Although every Worship Leader should be a devoted worshiper himself/herself, what are the downfalls of leading worship by only "modeling worship" to the congregation? Be as detailed as possible.

_____

_____

_____

_____

_____

_____

_____

_____

MORE TO THINK ABOUT:
KEEP LEARNING AND LEADING

To be an effective leader within the body of Christ, it is imperative for Worship Leaders to be lifelong learners. The more you learn, the more resources you'll have to encourage others in their worship of God. Consider what the Apostle Paul wrote to young Timothy: *"If you explain these things to the brothers and sisters, Timothy, you will be a worthy servant of Christ Jesus, one who is nourished by the message of faith and the good teaching you have followed"* (1 Tim 4:6, NLT). Resist the idea that you "have arrived" or know everything already. Be humble and keep learning!

4. Leading worship requires the leader to be intentional. Brooks provides two excellent examples: Road-maps for Worship[2] and the Worship Script.[3] Using one (or both) of these guideline methods, identify a specific worship service focus (a topic or Scripture passage) and then lay out an intentional worship service plan. Be specific and include the details.

_____

_____

_____

_____

_____

_____

_____

_____

Wisdom From The Early Church

"And now, my Lord, give to this your servant that which does not perish, preserving for us the spirit of your grace; and give us a share as you have filled us in the heart with worship in gentleness, as we glorify you through your Son, Jesus Christ . . ."

—APOSTOLIC TRADITION, 7.4

Take A Moment To Pray

Guide us with Your eye, O God

protect us with Your hand;

Renew us with Your words,

then send us out again.

In the name of the Father, and of the Son, and of the Holy Spirit.

Amen.

---

2. Brooks, Appendix 7.
3. Brooks, Appendix 8.

MY ACTION PLAN COMMITMENT

Here are the two ways I commit to use and apply what I have learned from chapter 15 in my life and/or ministry setting:

1. _____
   _____

2. _____
   _____

CHAPTER 16

Song Leader

"He who sings prays twice"

—ATTRIBUTED TO ST. AUGUSTINE

IN A CHURCH'S WORSHIP ministry, the Song Leader role is sometimes confused with that of the Worship Leader. The Song Leader's primary responsibility is to lead a congregation in their singing, encouraging them to participate in singing praise to God. Although it is an important aspect of worship, the singing of songs is only a small part of what worship fully encompasses. Whereas a Worship Leader leads and/or orchestrates a variety of worship expressions (prayer, confession, Scripture reading, dance, etc.) during a service, the Song Leader is focused on congregational singing.

1. What do both the Old and New Testaments specifically tell us about singing being a part of our faith?

_____

_____

_____

_____

_____

_____

_____

2. Why is singing out loud difficult for some people? What can we say and do to encourage others to sing to the Lord? Be specific.

_____

_____

_____

_____

_____

_____

_____

3. Why should we pay close attention to the lyrics of the songs we use in corporate worship?

_____

_____

_____

_____

_____

_____

_____

Back in chapter 12, Brooks introduced us to "an old Latin saying, *lex orandi, lex credendi*, which roughly means, the way in which we worship is the way in which we believe. Our worship is shaped by our beliefs and experiences." *What* we believe ends up shaping *how* we worship, and how we worship ends up shaping what we believe. Here in chapter 16, Brooks suggests a helpful adaptation: "*lex cantandi, lex credendi*—the way in which we sing is the way in which we believe." It is vital that we use songs during congregational worship that teach what the church should believe.

4. In the space provided below, write down the lyrics of one (1) contemporary worship chorus and then one (1) classic hymn, explaining in each case, *what* specific biblical/theological truths they teach us.

_____

_____

_____

_____

_____

_____

_____

5. Imagine that you have just been asked to step into the role of Song Leader for an upcoming worship service at the church you are currently attending. In order to help the congregation "find its voice," Brooks stresses you must take six specific questions into account. To the best of your ability answer each of these questions.

Who will make up the gathering?

_____

_____

_____

_____

_____

_____

_____

_____

What is their age range?

_____

_____

_____

_____

_____

_____

_____

_____

What are they used to singing in church?

_____

_____

_____

_____

_____

_____

_____

_____

What part does the music play in the flow of the service?

_____

_____

_____

_____

_____

_____

_____

_____

How might the Song Leader facilitate not only mood but also flow?

_____

_____

_____

_____

_____

_____

_____

How musically literate is the congregation?

_____

_____

_____

_____

_____

_____

_____

_____

6. Carefully and prayerfully read through Appendix 9. Select two (2) of John Wesley's "Directions for Singing" and explain *why* you believe them to be the *most* valuable and/or helpful.

_____

_____

_____

_____

_____

_____

_____

MORE TO THINK ABOUT: SINGING AS PRAYING

When a congregation sings to the Lord, they are often actually praying. Many of the hymns and choruses being sung today are actually prayers in the form of a song. It has been said that the Book of Psalms was ancient Israel's songbook. Although we're not sure of its origin, an oft-quoted saying is usually attributed to St. Augustine: "He who sings, prays twice." Song leaders in a church would do well to remember this connection between singing and praying in order to lead God's people in songs that make sense as appropriate expressions of prayer.

---

7. Carefully and prayerfully read through Appendix 10. Select four (4) of Brian Wren's "Guidelines for Encouraging Congregational Song" and explain *why* you believe these to be the *most* valuable and/or helpful.

_____

_____

_____

_____

_____

_____

_____

8. *What* does Brooks mean by "songs that are familiar," and *why* is it important to sing them?

_____

_____

_____

_____

_____

_____

_____

_____

9. *What* does it mean to sing songs that are "singable," and *why* is this important?

_____

_____

_____

_____

_____

_____

_____

_____

Wisdom From The Early Church

"Open, open your hearts to the exultation of the Lord, and let your love abound from the heart to the lips."

—*THE ODES OF SOLOMON, 8.1*

Take A Moment To Pray

Fill me, O Lord;

Fill my mind with awe and wonder;

Fill my heart with unconditional love;

Fill my mouth with prayers and praises

and what glorifies Your name.

Fill me, O Lord,

this day and every day.

Amen.

MY ACTION PLAN COMMITMENT

Here are the two ways I commit to use and apply what I have learned from chapter 16 in my life and/or ministry setting:

1. _____
   _____

2. _____
   _____

CHAPTER 17

Worship Artist

"Sing to him a new song; play skillfully, and shout for joy."

—*PSALM 33:3*

1. In this chapter, Brooks describes and defends the legitimacy of the Worship Artist. In your own words, explain why God calls some to be Worship Artists, and what sets them apart from whom some might consider ordinary worship musicians.

_____

_____

_____

_____

_____

_____

_____

2. Why might it not be a wise decision for a church to use a Worship Artist to lead their times of congregational worship?

_____

_____

_____

_____

_____

_____

_____

3. Describe the difference between *excellence* and *perfectionism* among Worship Artists and explain how church leaders should deal with both.

_____

_____

_____

_____

_____

_____

_____

_____

MORE TO THINK ABOUT:
USING ONE'S ARTISTIC TALENTS FOR WORSHIP

For well over 3,000 years, God has called on artists and craftsmen to use their gifts in ways that directly impact the worship of God by his people. In Exodus 35:10–19 we read, *"Let all the skilled artisans among you come and make everything that the Lord has commanded: the tabernacle. . . the altar. . .the anointing oil. . . the specially woven garments for ministering in the sanctuary. . ."* (HCSB). Later in Israel's history, *"David also ordered the Levite leaders to appoint a choir of Levites who were singers and musicians to sing joyful songs to the accompaniment of harps, lyres, and cymbals"* (1 Chron 15:16, NLT). Contributors to the worship of God are not limited to preachers, teachers, and worship leaders. Artists of all varieties have always been important to the Lord and remain so today.

---

4. Why do you suppose churches sometimes treat their Congregational Worship Gatherings as though they were Festival Worship Gatherings? Why might this be problematic? Be specific.

_____

_____

_____

_____

_____

_____

_____

_____

Wisdom From The Early Church

"Those who are wise in mind have a certain attribute of nature peculiar to themselves; and they who have shown themselves capable, receive from the Supreme Wisdom a spirit of perception in double measure. For those who practice the common arts, are in what pertains to the senses highly gifted ..."

—CLEMENT OF ALEXANDRIA, THE STROMATA, CHAPTER 4

Take A Moment To Pray

O Lord, You are the true Gift–Giver,

who blesses us with talents and abilities meant to bless and edify Your people.

I humbly ask You to bless the gifts You have given me.

May I worship with a passion, skill, and anointing

that truly blesses and strengthens Your people,

and brings You all the glory.

In the name of the Father, and of the Son, and of the Holy Spirit.

Amen.

MY ACTION PLAN COMMITMENT

Here are the two ways I commit to use and apply what I have learned from chapter 17 in my life and/or ministry setting:

1. _____

   _____

2. _____

   _____

CHAPTER 18

Worship Pastor

*"You aren't **just** a song leader. You aren't **just** a lead musician. Your set lists aren't **just** inspiring medleys of well–glued songs. You aren't merely on a stage, and those people out there aren't merely the audience. They are Christ's bride, God's beloved, gathered in from the four corners of the world that they might be reclaimed by and reaimed toward the Author and Perfector of their faith. They are disciples, followers. What you do and how you lead have a direct and formative impact on their journey of faith. Whether you know it or not, you are **pastoring** them."*[1]

—ZAC HICKS

THERE IS MOST LIKELY a good reason Brooks saved the role of the Worship Pastor for the final chapter.

1. Describe the priestly role of the Worship Pastor and explain how it is both similar to as well as different from the priesthood of all believers.

_____

_____

_____

_____

_____

_____

_____

2. In chapter 18, Brooks includes a list developed by Constance Cherry of important considerations regarding pastoral musicians. Of these seventeen considerations, select five (5) you believe are the most important and/or helpful in the ministry of the church, and explain why.

_____

_____

_____

_____

---

1. Hicks, *The Worship Pastor*, 13.

_____
_____
_____
_____

MORE TO THINK ABOUT:
SHEPHERDS AND PSALMISTS

Have you ever wondered why God chose David who was a shepherd boy (1 Sam 16:11–13), and then did a work in his life that resulted in his becoming the *"sweet psalmist of Israel"* (2 Sam 23:1)? Yes! David was a shepherd AND a psalmist—a pastor (the Greek word, poimēn, means both pastor and shepherd) AND a worship leader (see 2 Sam 6:12–21)! David certainly had his faults, and yet God used that pastor–worshiper to lead his people.

---

3. In what ways might a Worship Pastor impact the overall worship ministry of a church that Worship Leaders, Song Leaders, and Worship Artists likely would not? Be specific in providing your rationale.

_____
_____
_____
_____
_____
_____
_____

Wisdom From The Early Church

"Gather together frequently and seek those things that are good for your souls. Otherwise what use will having faith over all the time of your life be to you, if at the end of time you are not made perfect."

—*DIDACHE, 16.2*

Take A Moment To Pray

O God,

Thank You for lavishing Your unconditional love on me.

I would not be who I am or where I am

were it not for Your great and consistent love.

And now may that same love flow out of my life

to all whom You've graciously called me to lead and equip,

that together, we might magnificently magnify You

and give You the glory, honor, and praise You deserve;

In the name of the Father, and of the Son, and of the Holy Spirit.

Amen.

MY ACTION PLAN COMMITMENT

Here are the two ways I commit to use and apply what I have learned from chapter 18 in my life and/or ministry setting:

1. _____

   _____

2. _____

   _____

Conclusion

*"Worship changes the worshiper into the image
of the One worshiped"*

—JACK HAYFORD

1. Reread Psalm 77:11–14 and Mark 12:30. On a scale of 1–10, how would you rate yourself when it comes to personally being a wholehearted worshiper and why?

_____

_____

_____

_____

_____

_____

_____

_____

_____

_____

2. After reading *Worship Quest*, what aspects of personal and corporate worship are you most excited about developing further, and why?

_____

_____

_____

_____

_____

_____

_____

Wisdom From The Early Church

"The law instructs, history informs, prophecy predicts, correction censures, and morals exhort. In the Book of Psalms you find the fruit of all these, as well as a remedy for the salvation of the soul. The Psalter deserves to be called the praise of God, the glory of man, the voice of the Church, and the most beneficial confession of faith. The Psalms teach me to avoid sin, and to unlearn my being ashamed of repentance. In the Psalms delight and instruction vie with each other: we sing for enjoyment and read for instruction."

—AMBROSE (C. 339–397), BISHOP OF MILAN

Take A Moment To Pray
(Pray This Blessing Over Yourself)

May the All–Knowing One give you wisdom.
The All–Caring One send you aid.
The All–Forgiving One grant you pardon.
The All–Patient One help you wait.

May the All–Gracious One send you favor.
The All–Merciful One set you free.
The All–Righteous One make you more like him.
The All–Loving One change how you see.
In the Name of the Father, and of the Son, and of the Holy Spirit.
Amen.

www.ingramcontent.com/pod-product-compliance
Lightning Source LLC
Chambersburg PA
CBHW080600090426
42735CB00016B/3298